D1519688

**DELPHOS
LIBRARY**

DATE DUE	
APR 2 4 2003	

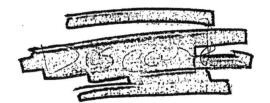

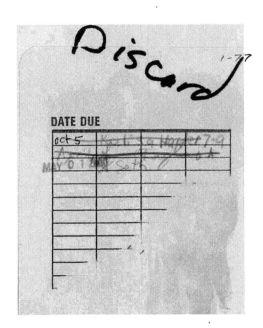

Discard

1-77

DATE DUE

oct 5			

919.69
Bia

HAWAII

in pictures

MINNEAPOLIS JUNIOR HIGH

Prepared by Lois Bianchi

VISUAL GEOGRAPHY SERIES

STERLING PUBLISHING CO., INC.   NEW YORK

Oak Tree Press Co., Ltd.
London & Sydney

VISUAL GEOGRAPHY SERIES

Afghanistan
Alaska
Argentina
Australia
Austria
Belgium and Luxembourg
Berlin—East and West
Bolivia
Brazil
Bulgaria
Canada
The Caribbean (English-Speaking Islands)
Ceylon (Sri Lanka)
Chile
China
Colombia
Costa Rica
Cuba
Czechoslovakia
Denmark
Dominican Republic
Ecuador
Egypt
El Salvador
England
Ethiopia

Fiji
Finland
France
French Canada
French Guiana
Ghana
Greece
Greenland
Guatemala
Guyana
Haiti
Hawaii
Holland
Honduras
Hong Kong
Hungary
Iceland
India
Indonesia
Iran
Iraq
Ireland
Islands of the Mediterranean
Israel
Italy

Jamaica
Japan
Jordan
Kenya
Korea
Kuwait
Lebanon
Liberia
Madagascar (Malagasy)
Malawi
Malaysia and Singapore
Mexico
Morocco
Nepal
New Zealand
Nicaragua
Nigeria
Norway
Pakistan and Bangladesh
Panama and the Canal Zone
Paraguay
Peru
The Philippines
Poland
Portugal

Puerto Rico
Rhodesia
Rumania
Russia
Saudi Arabia
Scotland
Senegal
South Africa
Spain
Surinam
Sweden
Switzerland
Tahiti and the French Islands of the Pacific
Taiwan
Tanzania
Thailand
Tunisia
Turkey
Uruguay
The U.S.A.
Venezuela
Wales
West Germany
Yugoslavia

PICTURE CREDITS

The publishers wish to thank the following organizations for the photographs used in this book: Dole Pineapple Company; John Graham and Company, Architects; Hawaiian Airlines; Hawaiian Visitors Bureau; Matson Navigation Company; Northwest Orient Airlines; Pan American World Airways; Sugar Research Foundation, Inc.; and United Airlines.

Fifteenth Printing, 1975
Copyright © 1973, 1971, 1968, 1967, 1966, 1965, 1961
by Sterling Publishing Co., Inc.
419 Park Avenue South, New York, N.Y. 10016
Distributed in Australia and New Zealand by Oak Tree Press Co., Ltd.,
P.O. Box J34, Brickfield Hill, Sydney 2000, N.S.W.
Distributed in the United Kingdom and elsewhere in the British Commonwealth
by Ward Lock Ltd., 116 Baker Street, London W 1
Manufactured in the United States of America
All rights reserved
Library of Congress Catalog Card No.: 61-10398
Sterling ISBN 0-8069-1006-2 Trade   Oak Tree 7061-6017 7
1007-0 Library

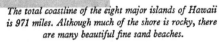

The total coastline of the eight major islands of Hawaii is 971 miles. Although much of the shore is rocky, there are many beautiful fine sand beaches.

CONTENTS

The volcanic origin of the islands is apparent in this view of the Iao Valley, a heavily foliaged gorge on Maui. Rising from its floor is the Iao Needle, a volcanic freak. The solid mass of this single stone stands 2,200 feet high.

INTRODUCTION

On March 18, 1959, Hawaii became the 50th of the United States of America. To many Americans, as well as non-Americans, Hawaii is known only from travel posters as a land of palm trees and pineapples, Waikiki Beach and the hula dance.

These are, of course, typical of Hawaii. The glorious scenery includes palm trees as well as exotic tropical flowers and luscious fruits. The pineapple, Hawaii's second most important export, is the result of modern agricultural methods and scientific canning factories. In turn, it provides a high rate of employment and the income for further technological research. Honolulu, capital of the state, is a thriving, energetic commercial city, its bustling port justly called "The Crossroads of the Pacific." And the hula, lovely vestige of ancient rituals, is a reminder of the old Polynesian way of life, pagan, peaceful, and pleasure-loving. Even the travel poster is meaningful, for tourism is the second most important source of income.

But posters certainly cannot picture all there is to see and know about Hawaii. Within its eight major islands are towering volcanic mountains, thick forests where ferns grow as tall as 40 feet, and gentle, rolling farmlands. There are beaches of sparkling white sand —and even one of jet black pulverized lava. There's the University of Hawaii, up to date in every way, as well as mysterious caves and ponds where elves and goddesses are said to have lived. These are Hawaii, too.

Extremely important is the lack of racial tension where members of several different races live side by side. Polynesians, Orientals and Caucasians—all have worked together to develop the islands, pooling the best of their respective abilities and talents.

Perhaps most of all, Hawaii is the land of *aloha*. The word itself connotes love, friendship, hospitality. And the spirit of *aloha* has been felt by every stranger in Hawaii from the early Polynesians, who were made welcome by the beauty of the islands themselves, through the explorers and missionaries to whom the islanders opened up their homes and their hearts, to every visitor lucky enough to make a trip to Hawaii today.

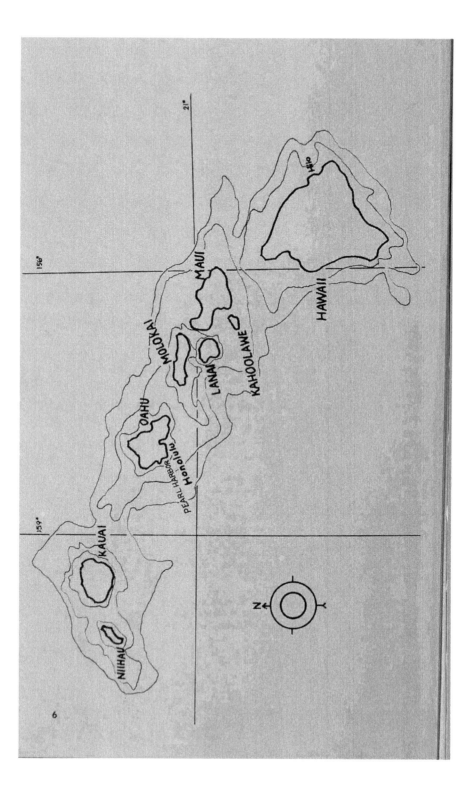

6

I. THE LAND

With the admission of its 50th state the United States has gained an island paradise: soft beaches, villas half-hidden among masses of flowers, flame trees, poinsettias, exquisite Chinese gardens, cascades of blossoms twined around tree trunks or tumbling into the sea, tall, splendid palms, their fronds swaying in the warm breeze, and beyond—everywhere in Hawaii—gleams the sea.

The 1,500-mile island chain known as Hawaii lies some 2,200 miles southwest of California, in the middle of the north Pacific Ocean. This group, the longest and one of the loveliest in the world, consists of eight islands large enough for habitation, and at least 16 others that are tiny, rocky and barren. The eight largest islands of Hawaii lie within a radius of 300 miles and have a total land area of 6,435 square miles—roughly the size of Connecticut and Rhode Island combined. These eight islands, which lie at the southeast end of the chain, form the State of Hawaii.

Hawaii is located within the northern margin of the Tropics. It occupies a position similar to that of Cuba in its geographic relation to the rest of the United States, which Hawaiians, proud and somewhat sensitive concerning their newly acquired statehood, refer to as "the mainland." From San Francisco visitors from the mainland can reach Honolulu, capital of the islands, in 4½ days by ship or just 4 hours by jet plane. Considering the rare beauty of the newest state, it is not at all surprising that an ever-increasing number are doing just that.

Of the group, the island called *Hawaii* is five times larger than any of the others and, in fact, is called the "Big Island" by Hawaiians. The most southeastern island of the chain, Hawaii is also sometimes called the "Orchid Island," for Hilo, the largest city and the major seaport of Hawaii, is the orchid-growing city of the world. The "Volcano Island" is Hawaii's third, and equally appropriate, nickname.

Hawaii was the most recently formed of the group, and of its four volcanoes, two—Mauna Loa and Mauna. Kilauea—are still active. Mauna Loa, second highest mountain in the islands, 13,675 feet, is not only the largest single mountain mass in the world, but also the world's largest active volcano. The most recent eruptions began on June 1, 1950 and lasted for 23 days. Although nowhere near so high as Mauna Loa, Kilauea is equally impressive. It erupted in 1959, 1961, and 1965. The 1961 eruption was remarkable for its three fountains spewing bright orange molten lava as high as 700 feet. But its most noted explosion occurred in 1790, when the native King Keoua was leading his army across its slopes. His march was interrupted by a fiery flow; the footprints of the men, as they tried in vain to escape the onrushing, red-hot stream, can still be seen in the hardened lava. During the 19th century, Kilauea erupted eight times.

Many of the Big Island's 62,464 inhabitants work at growing fruits, vegetables, coffee, macadamia nuts and, of course, the major crop, sugar. Forty per cent of the state's sugar is

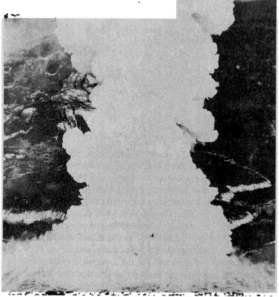

Left: The most recent eruption of Mauna Loa in 1950 sent rivers of molten lava cascading into the sea. By measuring the amount of lava which overflowed, geologists conclude that this eruption is the largest in historic times.

Below: Kilauea, one of the only two remaining volcanoes in Hawaii, has erupted at least a dozen times since records of the event were first kept in 1823. The crater, pictured here, is 4,000 feet above sea level and measures 8 miles in circumference.

More than 400,000 acres on the island of Hawaii are devoted to a National Park, thick with fern forests. Because of the great amounts of rainfall, some of these ferns reach heights of 40 feet.

raised on Hawaii. The island is best known and most remembered, however, for its magnificent scenic attractions. Here is the Hawaii National Park, the strangely beautiful result of centuries of volcanic activity, with its weird black rivers of hardened lava; great lava tubes (some big enough for a man to walk through); and powerful, hissing steam banks, caused by rain and ground water seeping down onto subterranean beds of still-hot rocks, thousands of feet below the earth's surface. Here, too, are vast rain forests, some 400,000 acres of them, where ferns may grow as tall as 40 feet, their stems as thick as tree trunks.

On Hawaii, too, in the Kona and Puna districts, are many fascinating relics of old Polynesia. The Kona coast is also the sports-fishing region of the islands. More than 650 species, including tunny, swordfish, barracudas, dolphins and bonitos, swim there all year around.

Maui, with a population of 36,000, is the second largest island. Its most important city is Lahaina, former capital of the islands and one-time whaling port. Because of its great double volcano, Maui is called the "Valley Isle" and is dominated in its larger section by the world's largest dormant volcano, Haleakala, the "House of the Sun." Haleakala is 25 square miles in area. The crater, 10,032 feet above sea level, is 20 miles in circumference and 2,000 feet deep. It is known in Polynesian folklore as the place where the demigod Maui snared the sun with his net and forced him to promise to pass more slowly over the mountain, because Maui's mother needed the sun's rays to dry the tapa cloth she was making.

Oahu, called the "Gathering Place," is the political, cultural and commercial core of Hawaii, for four-fifths of the total population of the islands or about 680,000 people, live here, most of them in or near the capital of Honolulu. Because it possesses two excellent landlocked

9

ports, Honolulu and Pearl Harbor, this island is the transportation base of the Pacific Ocean.

Oahu is 40 miles long and 26 miles wide. It consists of two lava-formed mountain ranges, the Waianae Range on the west, and on the east, forming the backbone of the island, the Koolau Range. These peaks abound in steep, rushing waterfalls and magnificent views of natural scenery.

The island of Oahu is best known for its military installations: Schofield Barracks, home of the 25th Infantry and until World War II the U.S. army's largest post; Wheeler Air Force Base, primary air communications base for the Pacific Command; and, of course, Pearl Harbor itself. The post was erected in a submerged valley, formed by the double estuary of the Pearl River, from which pearl-producing oysters were once taken in great quantities. The Hawaiians were uneasy when the base was first built, for legend tells that these waters are the home of the shark queen, a benevolent goddess who protects the waters from vicious, man-eating sharks. When in 1913 the first navy drydock collapsed just before its completion, some Hawaiians believed that angry sharks had pulled it down.

The collapse of this drydock preceded the much greater disaster which Pearl Harbor was to experience nearly 30 years later. On December 7, 1941, it was the site of one of the most devastating naval holocausts in history. The Japanese attack on American ships at Pearl Harbor, on planes at adjacent Hickam Field and at a nearby naval airfield was a national—indeed a world-wide—catastrophe. Inside of two minutes Japanese planes destroyed 33 American aircraft. Altogether, the United States lost 2,539 men, 185 planes and 18 ships; the Japanese fewer than 100 men, 29 aircraft, one large and 5 smaller submarines. This attack turned what had been a European war into a global war.

Today Pearl Harbor has been rebuilt. It is the most powerful naval base in the world. Visitors see endless stretches of masts, cranes and hangars, planes and battleships. Pearl Harbor is again peaceful, and like the rest of Oahu, it fairly hums with activity.

Next in size, *Kauai* is called the "Garden

Kalapana Beach in the Puna district of Hawaii island has a strange beauty all its own. An ancient lava flow which runs to the sea has been broken down through the centuries by the action of the surf, creating a soft sand that is jet black in color.

Standing on a pali, *or cliff, one can survey the entire island of Molokai. In the far distance is Kalaupapa, the Father Damien settlement devoted to the care of victims of leprosy.*

Isle." Indeed, it is perpetually green, and the name itself means "time of plenty" or "fruitful season." The island can boast of many "firsts" —the Polynesians, Captain Cook and the American missionaries all landed first at Kauai. Here, too, is the "wettest spot on earth"; the Kokee area has an average rainfall of 471.68 inches. In 1835 Hawaii's first sugar plantation, Koloa, was founded on Kauai.

The Garden Isle is lush, rich in canyons, valleys, waterfalls, plants and flowers of vivid hues. It supports a population of 28,035.

The "Friendly Island," with a population of 5,230 is *Molokai.* Off the northern coast of this island, and separated from it by a natural wall of rock 2,000 feet high, is the peninsula called Kalawao. Here stands Kalaupapa, a settlement for those afflicted with Hansen's disease, or leprosy. It was started by the Hawaiian govern-ment in 1866, but until the arrival in 1873 of Father Damien, a Roman Catholic priest from Belgium, conditions at Kalaupapa were ex-tremely inadequate. Largely because of Father Damien's appeals, the Hawaiian and U.S. governments contributed funds for hospitals and laboratories; today Kalaupapa is supported by the state government. Due to the develop-ment of sulphone drugs, Hansen's disease has been brought under control during the last 10 years, making it possible for visitors safely to go to the settlement. Most of Kalaupapa's 200 patients have been cured but many remain by choice on the "Friendly Island." On the main part of Molokai are two large pineapple plantations.

It is *Lanai,* however, next in size to Molokai, which is termed the "Pineapple Island." Lanai's 141 square miles are owned by The

First sight for visitors to Oahu is Diamond Head, a dormant volcano, guarding the entrance to Honolulu.

Waikiki Beach with its hotels and yacht basin lies under the shadow of Diamond Head, which here resembles a crouching lion in outline. The crater of this sleeping volcano, 77 acres in area, is now a National Guard Reservation.

Among the most useful trees found in Hawaii is the coconut palm. The nuts provide food and drink, the husks and shells make excellent bowls and containers and the palm fronds are used for weaving screens, matting and hats. The largest coconut grove on the islands provides shade for the black sand beach of Kalapana on Hawaii island.

Hawaiian Pineapple Company and are operated as a huge plantation. There are 2,267 inhabitants, nearly all of whom are supported by the pineapple industry.

The word "Lanai" actually means "swelling" or "hump" and is descriptive of the island's geographical shape. From the southern tip the land rises gradually to a height of 3,000 feet, from which it slopes downward again toward the northern tip.

Associated with Lanai is a curious story which is typical of the many legends still heard in Hawaii. Natives thought that this island was inhabited by ghosts and evil spirits for many hundreds of years after the Polynesians had settled in the other islands. Kaululaau, the nephew of the King of Maui, was banished to Lanai by his uncle as punishment for one of his pranks. Although Kaululaau was not expected to live, he proved his bravery by warring against the ghosts and evil spirits; he is believed to have made Lanai safe for human habitation.

Niihau is also surrounded with romance and legend. It is said to have been the original home of *Pele*, goddess of the volcanoes. Like Lanai, Niihau, smallest inhabited island, is privately owned. Located 17½ miles southwest of Kauai, Niihau has an area of only 72 square miles. The population: 243. Here, the Robinson family, the island's owners, maintain sheep and

13

cattle ranches and make every effort to preserve the peaceful, productive way of life typical of old Hawaii.

Uninhabited *Kahoolawe* is the smallest of Hawaii's eight major islands. Unlike the others, Kahoolawe is rocky and barren, totally unproductive; it is known as the "Island of Death." This is an appropriate name, for today Kahoolawe is used as a practice target for military bombardments.

TOPOGRAPHY

All eight islands are actually composed of mountaintops rising from one of the deepest sections of the Pacific Ocean. In total height these mountains are the highest in the world, rising 18,000 feet from the ocean floor to the water's surface and almost to 14,000 feet above the water in the case of the two most spectacular

Above: "Dripping," not "with jewels," but with orchids, this Hawaiian girl graciously displays Hawaii's best known symbol, the lei. The individual flowers are shaped and formed into strings by hand, and a single neckpiece may contain as many as 450 blossoms. Lei-making is one of the island's traditional arts.

Below: This barefoot Hawaiian girl is enjoying the view of palm-fringed Kailua Bay on the island of Hawaii. From this bay the sports-fishing boats put out in quest of marlin and other big game fish. Resort hotels line the far shore.

Mauna Kea, on the island of Hawaii, is the highest volcano in the 50th state, rising from the Kohala mountain range to a height of 13,796 feet. The ever-present clouds which surround it gave it the name "White Mountain." There is no record of Mauna Kea's last eruption, but the present state of its lava indicates that its final outburst probably occurred centuries ago.

peaks, Mauna Loa and Mauna Kea. In the winter these giants are snow-capped. However, the average elevation of the mountains comprising Hawaii is much below that of Mauna Loa and Mauna Kea; it is 2,000 feet above sea level.

According to Polynesian legend, the islands of Hawaii were fished up from the bottom of the

The crater of Haleakala, on the island of Maui, plays host to thousands of visitors on pack or hiking trips. The mountain slopes offer wonderful hunting in season, and all year-round the crater is a sight of rare beauty. Cinder cones in wonderful shades of red, orange, grey, lavender and black rise up from the crater floor. The exotic silversword plant, found nowhere else in the world, grows between these cones.

Above: The Hawaiian islands are the summits of the highest chain of mountains in the world, rising 18,000 feet from the ocean floor and extending upward as high as 13,796 feet above sea level. Shown here is the Waimea Canyon on the island of Kauai.

Left: The twin falls of Opaikaa, on Kauai, were named for the shrimp which ancient Hawaiians used to pluck from the rocks beneath the falls.

sea by Maui, who caught them in his net and tossed them about to rest in their present positions. Geologists, however, explain the formation of the islands this way: Millions of years before man appeared on earth a great rift opened up in the ocean floor. This crack, running from northwest to southeast, was at least 2,000 miles long, and through the centuries basalt lava bubbled up through it, eventually to form a colossal chain of mountains. The summits of these mountains are the islands of Hawaii.

The "Grand Canyon of the Pacific" is the name given to the rugged cliffs of the Waimea Canyon on Kauai. This lookout platform is one of many built just off the modern highway that almost completely encircles the island.

Interestingly, this geologic process still continues. Although only 2 of the 40 volcanic mountains in Hawaii are active, that activity is fairly frequent. Oddly enough, Hawaii is one place in the world where people run toward, not away from, volcanoes. The reason for this is that Hawaiian volcanoes are not at all violent—that is, as volcanoes go. Because the lavas are very fluid, gases contained in them can escape easily, and therefore do not build up pressures violent enough to result in terribly destructive explosions. Hawaiian volcanoes, in fact, rarely explode at all. Generally they "cough up"

Right: A most unusual geyser is Spouting Horn on the coast of Kauai. It is caused by the action of the waves dashing into the cavernous coastal rocks. The sound of each eruption can be heard for many miles on still, clear nights.

The peaceful Wailua River on the island of Kauai illustrates the topographical variety of the islands. The river valley is lush and verdant although it is surrounded by stony ridges. Along this river are a fern grotto and an historic place called the Wailua Birthstone, which mothers of the Hawaiian nobility always tried to reach in time for the birth of a child in order to ensure his future success and happiness.

Motorboat trips up the Wailua River are very popular with visitors to the Garden Isle, Kauai. The shores of the river are lined with dense forests and unusual trees of striking delicate beauty.

fluid basalt, which in most cases flows rather slowly, making it very easy for amateur photographers to capture the brilliant spectacle on film. These eruptions have taken place at least once a decade, and sometimes as often as every three or four years. Volcanologists in Hawaii are kept fairly busy predicting the next display from Mauna Loa.

In marked contrast to these current fireworks is the Punchbowl on Oahu. The oldest volcano on the islands, it has been dormant for more than 5,000 years. On this mountain, called the "Birthplace of Hawaii," is the site of the National Cemetery of the Pacific, where thousands of soldiers, sailors and marines, as well as the beloved war correspondent Ernie Pyle, lie buried.

CLIMATE

Hawaii is the U.S.A.'s only truly tropical state; its climate is the mildest and the extremes of temperature the narrowest in the United States.

"Perpetual spring"—this phrase truly describes the atmosphere of Hawaii where the temperature averages between 72° and 78° Fahrenheit in all seasons. The highest recorded temperature is 88°, the lowest 56°. Honolulu has an average of 286 days of sunshine or partial sunshine each year. The trade winds and the return ocean current from the Bering Straits are to be thanked for this. In general, the climate is so healthful that Hawaii is free of tropical diseases as well as of reptiles and disease-carrying and poisonous insects.

Rainfall is heavy in some localities. It is heaviest on the northwest mountain slopes. For example, Mt. Waialeale, on Kauai, the "wettest spot on earth," receives more than 470 inches of rain yearly. By contrast, the southern coasts of the islands get less than 9 inches, while the average rainfall in the cities amounts to less than 24 inches per year.

Hawaii is free from fog. The natural peace of the island is undisturbed by electrical storms or tornadoes. While earthquakes and tidal waves are not unknown, and have at times caused some damage, they are fortunately rare.

More varieties of orchids grow in Hawaii than anywhere else in the world. These are from an exhibit at Honolulu's Foster Botanical Garden, but the large commercial orchid-growing area is Hilo, on the island of Hawaii.

The only even slightly unpleasant feature of Hawaii's climate is that between September and April the *Konas* blow. These are variable winds, lasting from several hours to two or three days. However, even the Konas seem to bless the islands, for they always bring rain.

NATURAL RESOURCES

Rain might well be considered Hawaii's most precious natural resource. The soil, made up of decomposed lava enriched by vegetable humus, is extraordinarily fertile when it receives enough water. Since extensive irrigation systems have been put into use, water is now available nearly everywhere on the islands. The island of Oahu has an especially unique water supply. Because of the heavy rainfall, the porous soil and the thick forests, large bodies of fresh water accumulate under the central part of the island. This water gathers at sea level but is unable to escape to the sea because

19

the island is surrounded by impenetrable cap rock which imprisons it. The water is reached by drilling through the central part of the island. This great pool under Oahu, called the Ghyben-Hertzberg lens, supplies more than 50,000,000 gallons of fresh water daily from its seemingly inexhaustible supply. Since this water undergoes a natural purification, the addition of purifiers or water softeners is unnecessary.

By contrast, Hawaii is not rich in minerals, although bauxite and titanium were recently discovered. Building stone is abundant. Limestone is quarried on Oahu, and lava ash and rock with a high silicate content are found on all the islands. There are also limited deposits of clay which are used for ceramics and pottery.

But most seriously limited of all resources is land. Until 1848 a feudal system of landownership prevailed in Hawaii. In that year, the "Great Division" took place, forming the foundation of present land titles; 984,000 acres, or one-quarter of the total inhabited land, were set aside for the royal family, 1,500,000 acres for the government, and nearly 1,750,000 acres were divided among the several tribal chiefs. The common people received 28,600 acres and titles to the land they cultivated and lived on. In most cases, the tribal chiefs died in debt, very often without heirs, and their land fell into the hands of the many economically farsighted foreigners who had come to Hawaii. When the monarchy was abolished in 1893, the lands of the crown were made public. They were turned over to the United States in 1898

Natives of Kauai are taking part in a hukilau, *a community net-pulling. This monthly fishing festival, dating from ancient times, still provides keen sport and a fine catch for eating. One large net is laid and trimmed with leaves whose shadows are supposed to frighten the fish into the circle. Everyone who* hukis, *or pulls the net gets a share of the catch. One part of the old custom not followed today was to celebrate a successful* hukilau *with a luau.*

when Hawaii was annexed. Today, the state and federal governments own more than 40 per cent of the total area of the inhabited islands. Although they occasionally lease portions of this land, most of it is maintained for state and national parks and for defence purposes. Even further limiting the possibilities of buying land in Hawaii is the fact that of the land which is privately owned, only four people, each with over 100,000 acres of land, own one-third of it, and another twelve people, each with over 30,000 acres, own another third.

VEGETATION

Because of Hawaii's warm climate, heavy rainfall and fertile soil, trees and plants grow in great abundance and variety. There is a plentiful supply of wood, for trees in Hawaii grow two to three times as fast as they do in other areas of the United States. Among the many kinds of tropical and subtropical plants, the most important is probably the taro shrub,

The fishing is excellent on Oahu. Tanned and happy, visitors to Hawaii enjoy surf casting from the rough KoKo Head shore of the island. The fine white sand of this beach is quite a contrast to the jet black sand of Kalapana on Hawaii island.

from which *poi,* the Hawaiian "staff of life," is made. *Poi* is a starchy, pudding-like food, made from taro roots by steaming, peeling and pounding them into a purple-tinted, pasty substance. The ti leaf plant is also extremely useful. Used as a medicine by the ancient Hawaiians, today the leaves are used to make such items as tablecloths and hula skirts. A parchment made from the ti leaf is also used in Polynesian cookery; fish is wrapped in it before being steamed. In addition to sugar cane and pineapple, which are cultivated for commercial uses, mangoes, papayas, bananas, avocados, tamarinds and custard apples grow in abundance and require little care.

21

The silversword, so called because of the silver color of its thin, bladelike leaves, is a rare plant found only in the Haleakala Crater on the island of Maui. When the plant is several years old, it bursts into bloom with hundreds of purple and yellow flowers. After a single blooming the plant dies, but, fortunately, new ones are coming up all the time.

Not including leis, those lovely, long floral wreaths which have symbolized Hawaii since ancient Polynesian days, more than 500,000 packages of flowers and foliage are exported from Hawaii each year. Growing on the islands are at least 900 different types of flowering trees and shrubs. Poinciana, jacaranda, Bougainvillia, oleander and the African tulip are only a few. Particularly interesting is the night-blooming cereus, whose flowers are coaxed forth by the light of the moon. The islands abound in familiar flowers—orchids, roses, gardenias, carnations—as well as in vivid, exotic ones such as hibiscus, red lehua, klina and mokihana.

Here, too, are many different kinds of birds and animals. The slopes of Mauna Kea, Hawaii's most magnificent peak, are a hunter's paradise. Among others, he will find pheasants, California valley quail, Japanese quail, barred and lace-neck doves, wild pigeons and chukar partridges. Flourishing on the islands are more than 150 species of song birds, game birds and ornamental birds, about a fourth of which are immigrants from Asia and Australia.

Everything thrives, for Hawaii is a garden. Its fascinating geological structure, soothing climate, brilliantly exotic flowers and trees make this state a spot of unforgettable beauty and harmony, a veritable Eden.

The hibiscus is the official flower of the state of Hawaii. Nearly 5,000 different varieties of this beautiful flower grow on the islands. The hibiscus blooms all year round.

22

The shores of Kauai (seen here), Oahu and the southern part of Molokai are lined with coral reefs, built up over the centuries by accumulations of the bodies of tiny coral animals who died there. Oddly, these reefs are nearly absent from the islands of Hawaii and Maui.

2. HAWAII'S HISTORY

The true story of the first discovery of Hawaii will probably remain a matter of dispute forever. Recorded history begins with the landing of British Captain James Cook in 1778, but stories persist, some legendary, some true, concerning the original discovery of the islands.

The most ancient legend tells that the first man to see the islands was a Polynesian fisherman and navigator from the South Seas named Hawaiiloa. Other Polynesian myths concern a race of elves called *menehunes*, said to have settled on Hawaii in A.D. 400. A most industrious group, these elves worked only in the dark of night, supposedly using a series of eerie caves on the island of Kauai as their daytime hiding place. There are several old fish ponds and other waterworks on the island which are still pointed to as proof of the menehunes' existence.

Actually, the waterworks were probably built by Polynesians, known to have come to Hawaii between the 8th and 11th centuries. It is believed that these Polynesians, like the

This dark and mysterious cavern on the island of Kauai is said to have been a hiding place for the menehunes, mythical elves who supposedly first settled in Hawaii. Other legends say that these caves were the gathering places of ancient Hawaiian chieftains who held secret conclaves there.

legendary Hawaiiloa, came from Tahiti, having sailed their big double canoes 2,676 miles northward across the Pacific. The migration of the Polynesians is an astonishing navigational feat. Their gigantic canoes were made of sections of hardwood bound together with ropes of coconut fibre and propelled by square sails consisting of very large leaves. Since the canoes were uncovered, the seafaring Polynesians had no protection from winds and rain and, of course, no "ports during a storm." We will never know how many started or how many reached Hawaii, but it is certain that many Polynesians must have perished on this dangerous voyage.

Each 98-foot canoe carried 60 persons and was similar to the Malayan outrigger. These craft were extremely speedy, seaworthy and manoeuvrable, and could sail close to the wind. To survive, the Polynesians must have carried fresh water, provisions and many other supplies to supplement the fish they caught as they travelled. Pigs, chickens and many of the plants now found in Hawaii were brought to their new land by the Polynesians.

The first European claim to a discovery of Hawaii comes from Spain. Juan Gaetano, a Spanish navigator, supposedly arrived at Hawaii in 1555 and named the islands "La Mesa," the "tableland." The fact that the position of Hawaii is correctly marked on Spanish navigational charts of the late 16th century tends to substantiate this claim.

Fully documented facts about Hawaii, however, did not exist until 1778 when the noted English explorer, Captain Cook, came upon the islands accidentally. Cook was on a voyage from England, sponsored by the Earl of Sandwich, in search of the Northwest Passage. The first English name given to Hawaii, the Sandwich Islands, was Cook's way of paying homage to his patron. Captain Cook was warmly received by the Polynesian natives who took him for a god. Cook did nothing to discourage this misconception. It is hinted, in fact, that he took gross advantage of the natives because of it. However, on his second voyage to Hawaii in 1779, a dispute arose over some supposedly stolen goods, and Cook's men attacked an Hawaiian chief. In the ensuing battle, the English captain was stabbed to death. For several years following Cook's death, very few foreign vessels approached the islands' shores.

Within the islands themselves important social and political changes were taking place during the 18th century. But in order to understand these changes, we must know something of how the early Hawaiians lived. When Captain Cook arrived, each island was an independent kingdom, ruled by its own chief. There existed a rigid class system which the Polynesians had brought with them from Tahiti.

This system was headed by the *alii*, chiefs and nobles who were called the "Lordly Ones" because of their supposed descent from the gods, in conjunction with the *kahuna*, or priests. The chiefs owned all the land while the *makaainana*, or workers, lived in a serf-like state of poverty and suppression. The *alii* used their claim of divine origin to terrify and oppress the common people. Women occupied an inferior social position; polygamy—a system under which each man is permitted to have more than one wife—was the accepted way of life in old Polynesia. The chiefs married their closest relatives, and infanticide was their way of eliminating any defective children which resulted from these inbred marriages.

The Polynesian religion, which was important in maintaining the class structure, was a form of nature worship involving many gods. Chief among these gods were *Kane*, the lord of creation in whose abode lived the souls of all chiefs; *Ku*, the god of war; *Lono*, god of the earth; and *Pele*. Goddess of fire, *Pele* was thought to cause volcanic eruptions. She was so greatly feared that no Polynesian ever approached a volcanic crater without bringing an offering. When an eruption threatened, the frightened people rushed to appease *Pele* by

Several villages in Hawaii feature replicas of ancient Hawaiian hales, or houses. These houses were made of wood, then thatched with ferns, grass and leaves. The visitors shown here are receiving leis, floral garlands symbolic of Hawaiian hospitality.

25

This bronze statue of Kamehameha stands in front of the Department of Justice Building in Honolulu's Civic Center. The statue commemorates the day the King stood, dressed in a magnificent cloak and helmet made of feathers, on the cliffs of the northern coast of Hawaii and surveyed the largest fleet ever assembled in the islands. These warrior ships had been summoned by the supposedly magic kihapu, *a conch shell studded with the teeth of conquered chiefs. Kamehameha stretched out his arm over these white-sailed canoes, and sent them out to begin the conquest of Maui and Oahu.*

throwing animals, fruits and fish into volcanic craters. Not only eruptions, but all natural phenomena were explained by the priests as the work of the gods. Each god was represented by an idol to which human lives were sometimes sacrificed.

Another feature of the Polynesian religion was the belief in the survival of the soul after death. According to the *kahuna*, the soul first wandered around the body of the deceased, haunted dark, mysterious places and even haunted its enemies. Later it withdrew to the dwelling of the god, *Wakea*, the legendary father of the Hawaiians. If the deceased had obeyed the sacred laws, his soul lived after him in a state of pleasure and joy; otherwise, it was hurled down a precipice to a region of torment and despair called *Milu*.

The most important characteristic of Polynesian life was the *tabu*. The word itself means "forbidden," and there was a vast network of *tabus*, minute regulations covering every aspect of life. Many *tabus* affected women in particular; for example, they were prevented from eating certain foods and from eating with men. Many *tabus* were completely unreasonable. If the shadow of a common man touched the body of a Lordly One, even by accident, the punishment was death. A man would meet the same fate if he came into the home of a chief without having been summoned. Until the 19th century the *tabus* were fanatically observed by *alii* and *makaainana* alike, for the breaking of one of these rules was the most serious of all possible crimes and punishable by death. The *kahuna* who enforced the system of *tabus* used them to keep the people in a state of fear, thereby to maintain and increase their own power.

The *alii*, too, were constantly struggling to achieve more power, and wars between the different tribes were very frequent. One of the northern tribes on the island of Hawaii was ruled by a young chief named Kamehameha, who in later years was known as "The Great" and "The Napoleon of the Pacific." In 1791, Kamehameha started a prolonged war which ultimately made him master of all the islands. His most famous conquest was the battle of Nuuanu Pali on Oahu. There the warrior king forced thousands of enemy soldiers into a narrow gorge and over a high precipice to meet death on the rocks below. With this victory, Kamehameha accomplished his goal, and by 1810 the islands were unified under his leadership.

Kamehameha the Great died in 1819. When his son Kamehameha II took over the throne, many chiefs and priests were agitating for the overthrow of the *tabu* system. The people were growing tired of being oppressed by the *tabus*, and many no longer believed in the power of their gods. The king himself was openly sceptical, and one day made up his mind to put a *tabu* to the test. One of the most serious restrictions forbade men and women to eat together. One afternoon when lunch was served at the palace, the king left his own table, sat down with the women of the court and completed his meal with them. The court was aghast— especially when absolutely nothing happened as a result. Word of this great event spread rapidly among the Hawaiian people.

A somewhat different version of how the *tabus* were overthrown gives the credit to Princess Keopuolani, one of the wives of Kamehameha I. She is believed to have led a feminist revolt against the *tabus*, many of which were particularly oppressive to women. It is said that on the night Kamehameha I died, this princess publicly ate the nut of the forbidden coconut, offering to share it with the chiefs who were present. It is she, according to this account, who later persuaded the new king, Kamehameha II, to set a precedent by eating with the noble women of the court. Regardless of whether he was prompted by Princess Keopuolani, it is certain that Kamehameha II struck the most serious single blow to the *tabu* system by eating publicly with women. Within the next few months all *tabus* were abolished, temples and idols destroyed.

Since the priests and *alii* who opposed the old way had nothing to offer in its place, Hawaii for a time became largely a land without a religion. However, thousands of Polynesians quietly clung to the belief that there was a single "true god." This idea was attributed to the legendary Hawaiiloa, who, it was said, had prophesied that the true religion would one day come to the islands in the form of a square

black box. The square black box was later interpreted as the English Bible, and indeed the events of the next 50 years seemed to prove the truth of Hawaiiloa's words.

The Bible was brought to Hawaii by a group of devoted, hard-working, courageous Protestant ministers from New England. On April 4, 1820, the first mission arrived from Boston aboard the brig *Thaddeus,* under the auspices of the American Board of Commissioners of Foreign Missions. Interestingly enough, these missionaries were sent at the instigation of a native Hawaiian. In 1817 young Henry Obookiah went to the United States as a stowaway on a ship. The captain of the ship befriended the boy and took him to his home in New Haven, Connecticut. There, Obookiah met the Reverend E. W. Dwight of Yale University, who soon converted him to Christianity. Obookiah studied at the Foreign Mission School in Cornwall, Connecticut, along with four other Hawaiian boys. During that year he made many public speeches, emphasizing the sin and darkness in which his fellow Hawaiians were living and painting an apparently exaggerated picture of their wretchedness. He continually urged the sending of missionaries to his homeland, and just after his death in 1819 the first group was dispatched.

Above and below: Hulihee Palace at Kona, on the island of Hawaii, was once the summer retreat of Hawaiian royalty. From the verandas, former kings enjoyed the view across Kailua Bay to the sea beyond. Today it is a museum, welcoming thousands of visitors each year.

Lahaina on the island of Maui was the capital of Hawaii under Kamehameha II. Old cannon guard the quiet waterfront, once a busy port of call for whaling ships. Pioneer Inn, in the background, has been restored to its 19th-century appearance.

On the *Thaddeus* were 7 missionary couples, 5 children and 3 Hawaiian youths from the Cornwall School, who served as assistants and interpreters. During the next 25 years, 11 more boatloads arrived in Hawaii, bringing about 125 more missionaries; at least another 30 came to live in the islands before the end of the 19th century.

The missionaries, all well-educated and dedicated people, learned the Hawaiian language and continued the work of translating the Bible into that tongue, a project which had been started by Obookiah. The missionaries began their work by teaching the chiefs to read, and by 1824 they had taught at least 2,000 natives to read their own language. They also started English schools for their own children which the Hawaiians, too, eventually attended. The first Christian church was opened in 1821. Since many Hawaiians were eager to adopt a new religion and many of the *alii* converted quickly, the Christianizing of Hawaii was rapidly accomplished.

In addition to their religious work, the missionaries established hospitals, libraries and a newspaper. With a firm conviction that all souls were equal before God, they taught the natives the meaning of democracy and brought about the gradual Americanization of the islands.

Life was very hard for the missionaries in Hawaii. Their salaries were extremely low and their hours long. Ironically, many of their problems came from their fellow Americans. The white sailors who docked at the islands never missed a chance to make fun of, or create trouble for, the missionaries. One of the sailors' major objections was that the missionaries imposed their own strict Puritan morality on the relaxed, easy-going Polynesians.

The American Protestants, of course, were

29

not the only missionaries who came to Hawaii. In 1827, a Roman Catholic priest from France, an Irish priest and several missionary workers were sent to the islands by Pope Leo XII. Other Jesuit priests followed during the next 50 years. In general, the Catholic missions were not as large nor apparently as effective as those established by Protestant groups.

Just as the religious structure of the islands was undergoing change, so was its social and political makeup. About 1850, large numbers of Chinese were brought to Hawaii to work on the plantations. But since the Chinese quickly attained higher economic and social positions, so new workers were needed. In 1885 Japanese began coming to Hawaii, only to be succeeded, as they too improved their way of life, by still other groups of immigrants.

In 1839, King Kamehameha III signed a Bill of Rights, guaranteeing civil liberties to the Hawaiian people for the first time in their history. Soon afterwards, in 1840, the first constitution was adopted. In 1842, a uniform code of laws was formulated, and in 1845 the first Hawaiian legislature met. In 1852 a second and still more liberal constitution was signed, giving the right to vote for members of the legislature to all adult males. The legal code was altered to provide consistently impartial laws for all inhabitants of the islands, including those who were citizens of other countries. With the death of Kamehameha V in 1872, his great dynasty came to an end, and the legislature, using the powers provided by the constitution, elected first Lunalilo and then Kalakaua as king.

King Kalakaua tried to restore an autocratic government, but he was compelled by the legislature to limit his powers. In 1891 he was succeeded by his sister, Liliuokalani, who also tried to re-establish an absolute monarchy. In 1893, Liliuokalani attempted to abolish the constitution, but she was defeated by the Constitutional Party. The Queen was dethroned and the legislature set up a provisional government in the form of a republic. The elected officials of this republic were mostly American; this was natural enough since the monarchy had long been appointing Americans to top ministerial and other government posts. In

The official seal of the state of Hawaii has changed only slightly since the days when it was the symbol of the monarchy. The motto remains the same. Translated, it reads, "The Life of the Land Is Preserved in Righteousness."

1894, Sanford B. Dole was elected the first President of Hawaii.

No history of Hawaii would be complete without the story of Sanford Ballard Dole, "the grand old man of Hawaii." Honolulu-born, Dole was a leader of the movement which ended the monarchy in 1893, leader of negotiations to make Hawaii a part of the United States, first and only President of the Republic of Hawaii, and first Governor of the Territory after annexation.

In 1840 Dole's parents came to Hawaii from Maine to take charge of the Punahou School at which young Sanford, born in 1844, was educated. At age 21, Dole attended Williams College in Massachusetts, then went on to study law in Washington, D.C. After being admitted to practice in 1867, he returned to Hawaii, where he took a leading role in politics. He was elected to the Hawaiian legislature in 1884, and two years later was appointed Associate Justice of the Hawaiian Supreme Court, where he served for 6 years. In the difficult first years of the Republic, Dole acted with great wisdom, tact and diplomacy, qualities which served him and Hawaii well in his efforts to make it a part of the United States.

He served as Governor of the Territory until 1903 when he was appointed United States District Judge, in which capacity he served until 1916. Dole was elected President of the Hawaiian Bar Association, and served in his later years as a member of a committee to recommend legislation on Hawaii to Congress. Truly one of the makers of Hawaii's history, Dole died in 1926.

One of the first acts of the new Republic established by the defeat of Queen Liliuokalani was to negotiate an annexation treaty for Hawaii with the United States. President Benjamin Harrison was considering the step in February, 1893, just prior to the close of his administration, but his successor, Grover Cleveland, was entirely unsympathetic to Hawaiian annexation. The determined islanders brought the treaty up again during William McKinley's administration, and on July 7, 1898, Hawaii was annexed to the United States by a joint resolution of Congress. Later in 1900,

Hawaii received the status of a territory, an area "on probation" until it could be considered ready for full statehood. It was then that Sanford B. Dole was appointed Governor of the new territory.

As an American territory, Hawaii lacked many of the privileges of a state. Although the Hawaiians elected a delegate to the House of Representatives, he could only take part in debate and was not allowed to vote. Hawaiians could not elect their own governor or their own judges. These officials were appointed by the President of the United States. Although Hawaiians paid federal taxes and came under the jurisdiction of the United States Constitution and federal laws, they were not yet allowed to vote in Presidential elections.

Small wonder then, that the Hawaiians were so anxious to be admitted to full statehood. The first official bill toward that end was submitted to Congress by the Hawaiian legislature in 1903. This bid proved unsuccessful, as did at

Iolani Palace in Honolulu, once the home of Hawaii's kings, and later the state capitol of Hawaii contains the only throne room in the U. S. It is open to visitors when it is not in use as a session chamber for the state House of Representatives. The ceremony of annexation to the United States took place at Iolani Palace.

31

least 16 others. In all, some 34 bills concerning Hawaii's statehood were introduced, and defeated, in Congress. Dozens of Congressmen visited the islands, hundreds of witnesses testified at official hearings. The House of Representatives passed the statehood bill three times, but it always bogged down in the Senate, either in a tangle of committee rules, or because of Senate efforts to combine it with an Alaskan statehood bill.

Finally, in 1959, a Hawaiian statehood bill was passed by both houses of Congress. Amidst great rejoicing and a carnival-like celebration, the bill was overwhelmingly ratified by the Hawaiians on March 18 of that year. Now, like the other states, the 50th and newest has two senators, sends one delegate to the House of Representatives, elects its own governor, lieutenant governor and judges. The state constitution of Hawaii is patterned after the U.S. federal constitution.

The new state includes the eight main islands, but not the far-flung atolls of the chain, which remain federal territory.

A higher percentage of registered voters go to the polls on election day in Hawaii than in any other state in the Union.

The new state capitol in Honolulu is a five-storey structure surrounded by a giant pool.

Built on the rusting hulk of the battleship "Arizona" in Pearl Harbor, this simple concrete structure is visited by many thousands each year. Inside, the military guard stands watch over a marble wall, listing the names of the "gallant men here entombed and their shipmates who gave their lives in action on December 7, 1941."

3. THE PEOPLE

The most dynamic—and most typically American—factor of life in Hawaii is the mixture of races, nationalities and cultures that makes up its population. As in the rest of the United States, the citizens of the state of Hawaii hail from many different racial backgrounds. But Hawaii is far ahead of many of the other states in solving racial problems. One Hawaiian way of eliminating racial discrimination is by eliminating racial differences, for there marriage between the races is extremely common. Since World War II one out of every three marriages in the 50th state has been interracial, and it is estimated that by the end of this century, fully half the population will be of mixed blood. Another force which has broken down racial barriers in Hawaii has been the growth of a middle class, in which both whites and Asians have attained the same social and economic standing.

Hawaii's population of 880,000 is divided into three major racial divisions: Polynesian, Oriental and Caucasian. Although archaeologists believe the islands were inhabited as early as A.D. 124, the first settlers about whom anything is known are the Polynesians who came between the 8th and 11th centuries. These people probably originated in the East Indies many, many centuries before migrating to Tahiti and, from there, to Hawaii. They were not savages, for they had stone-cutting implements and tools for cultivating the soil. They built houses of wood and thatched them with leaves, grass and ferns; they possessed huge sailing canoes, and they wore clothes made from dried tapa leaves. They fished and raised taro, sweet potatoes, coconuts, bananas, and sugar cane for their food.

At the time Captain Cook discovered the Hawaiian islands in 1778, there were more than 400,000 Polynesians living there. In the century that followed, however, Western diseases,

On special occasions and for festivals Hawaii's Japanese citizens dress in native costumes. These girls wear elaborately decorated silk kimonos, their sleeves falling nearly to the ground and obis, the traditional Japanese sashes.

against which the natives had no immunity, caused so many deaths that there were only 58,000 Polynesians left in 1878.

This sharp decrease in population, combined with the growth of large sugar plantations started in the islands by Americans, resulted in a severe worker-shortage in Hawaii. By 1850, therefore, the plantation owners were actively trying to interest workers from other countries in emigrating to Hawaii. It was primarily for this reason, to work in the sugar cane fields, that so many different peoples came together, making Hawaii, as well as the mainland, a "melting pot."

Beginning in 1852, plantation owners brought over many workers from China. First to arrive, the Chinese were also first to leave the plantations and go to the towns to open shops, work as clerks, start rice-growing farms and to acquire property. The Chinese were particularly concerned with educating their children, and today, with most of them living in Honolulu, the Chinese number among the wealthiest and most influential people on the islands. Within the last 25 years there has been a gradual moving away from traditional attitudes, particularly ancestor worship. As very strict parental authority has decreased, the traditional Oriental custom of families arranging marriages has lost out, and intermarriage with other races has increased. Although there are 100 Buddhist temples in Hawaii, this religion is no longer very strong, except among the older generation. Like all Hawaiians, the Chinese have become more and more Americanized.

In 1885, after many Chinese had left the plantations, Japanese workers were brought to Hawaii to take their place. Today, many Japanese are in white collar jobs, in fishing and in crafts. Many others have gone into service industries, such as cleaning, plumbing, mechanics, dressmaking and tailoring. Japanese farmers in Hawaii today are the principal growers of coffee and flowers. A small number have also become merchants and shopkeepers. Like the Chinese, the Japanese insist on education for their children. As a result, a growing number of the younger generation are prominent in the professions and in politics.

These lovely Hawaiian girls reflect the diversity of their racial background. Although there are three major racial groups in Hawaii—Polynesian, Oriental and Caucasian—intermarriage is extremely common.

Between 1905 and 1914, Portuguese, Spaniards and Filipinos came to Hawaii to work on the sugar plantations. The Portuguese arrived in family groups, unlike the previous all-male contingents of Orientals who sent for wives only after several years on the islands. Most Portuguese have stayed on the plantations, although some of the younger ones have moved to the cities to learn semiskilled trades like stone masonry and typography. A few have gone into professions. The Filipinos, who are mainly of Malay stock, with a touch of Spanish, are the last large group to have come to Hawaii. Their work is still the mainstay of the sugar plantations, although Filipinos, too, are slowly seeking other kinds of work.

In addition to these larger groups of immigrants, smaller numbers of Russians, Koreans, Germans, Scandinavians, Puerto Ricans and South Sea Islanders have settled in Hawaii, making it a truly cosmopolitan state. It is also a youthful state, with more than half the population under 24 years of age; immigration is

responsible for this, too. Until Hawaii became a state and acquired United States immigration restrictions, people from other countries were encouraged, as we have seen, to emigrate. Young people made up the bulk of the immigrants, for the work ahead would be hard. Today it is the children of these young immigrants who are swelling the rolls of Hawaii's population.

Throughout this influx of new peoples, the original Hawaiians have perhaps fared the worst economically. Polynesians now work mostly in the tourist trades, as civil servants, police, firemen and construction workers. Of all the racial groups, they have intermarried the most freely. Today a pure Polynesian is extremely rare in Hawaii. Even the simple and lovely Polynesian language is rarely heard, for of course English is the dominant tongue, having been taught exclusively in Hawaiian schools since 1893.

The similarity of the old Hawaiian language to that of Tahiti is one of the most important factors supporting the widely held belief that this is where the early Hawaiians lived before their migration. The original Polynesian language had only twelve letters: A E H I K L M N O P U W. Because of the frequency of vowels in relation to that of the harder consonants, Hawaiian has a soft, musical quality. Traces of this tongue are heard in Hawaii today mixed with English in the strange dialect called "Pidgin." This is spoken by the less well-educated Polynesians, especially for the benefit of tourists. Ladies are always charmed to hear themselves called *wahine* (Hawaiian for woman), while men are addressed as friend.

Hawaii is the first U.S. state whose people are predominantly of Asian origin, and it has had its racial problems. But the 50th state can be justly proud of the way in which it has solved them. Generally, the whites or *haoles* tend not to intermarry or to mix socially with the other races, and in some fields they enjoy better job opportunities than do other Hawaiians. Nevertheless, any segregation or discrimination is illegal and practically nonexistent. Of course there are some tensions, especially felt by the Filipinos, who are the latest arrivals and have not yet had time to become thoroughly ab-

35

A typical small, rural church is this one at Kapaa on the island of Kauai. Youngsters of half a dozen different races may attend any single church here.

sorbed into the life of the islands. But, in general, there is equality in housing, employment, education, social and recreational facilities, business and civic affairs. There are representatives of all the races among those who have risen to wealth and prominence in every field.

In religious matters Hawaiians have also proved themselves tolerant and open-minded. Hawaii has more than 400 Protestant churches, 115 Catholic parishes, 100 Buddhist temples, 1 Mormon temple and 1 Jewish synagogue. This diversity occurs even within single families whose members may belong to different religious groups. The emphasis on interfaith cooperation is very strong. The Church of the Crossroads in Honolulu is a perfect example of the interracial, interreligious attitude in Hawaii. Here, Western furnishings grace a Chinese

court with Oriental pillars carved from Hawaiian woods. Like the state itself, this church has utilized the best of several cultures in order to achieve its own particular beauty and character.

Similarly, holidays and festivals in the islands reflect the rich and varied traditions of their citizens. As on the mainland, New Year's Eve and the Fourth of July are occasions for dazzling fireworks, boisterous parades and general merrymaking. But most Hawaiian holidays would not seem so familiar to Westerners as these. The Chinese community celebrates the new year, as determined by a special lunar calendar, with a gala Narcissus Festival. This includes a parade in which fantastic replicas of animals are carried, and there are unicorn dances, a Chinese play, flower shows and the selection of a festival queen. In autumn the Chinese hold an equally lively Moon Festival.

Above: A Buddhist priest in front of his temple on Kauai is a reminder of an Asian contribution to the state. There are today 100 such Buddhist temples in Hawaii, although their members are almost exclusively of the older generation.

Below: The Mormon Temple in Laie, a suburb of Honolulu, is the largest one west of Salt Lake City, Utah. It is sometimes called the "Taj Mahal of Hawaii."

Except for the palm trees, this might be a sleepy New England town. The influence of the American missionaries is clearly seen in the architecture of the Central Union Church. Located in the Makiki section of Honolulu, the lawns and walks of the church are shaded by monkeypod trees and palms. The smaller building is the more recent Atherton Chapel.

Hawaii's Buddhist citizens commemorate the birth of Gautama Buddha on Wesak Day, the nearest Sunday to April 8th. Native costumes are worn, and there are many ritualistic dances, truly fascinating to visitors who have never before seen them. Other musical celebrations are held by the Buddhists every weekend during July and August for the purpose of paying tribute to the dead. A striking cultural contrast is the Fiesta Filipina, usually held in mid-June. Hawaiians of Philippine origin recall a chosen patron saint with vivid dances to the music of string bands and a series of unusual athletic events. Still other Hawaiian holidays are Lei Day, the 50th State Fair, Kamehameha Day, the Hula Festival and Aloha Week.

EDUCATION

The story of education in the state of Hawaii is also the story of the successful struggle for racial equality. Education began in 1840 when King Kamehameha III asked the American missionaries to establish a free, compulsory school system, whereby each community would be required to maintain a school. This occurred 45 years before the United States took the same important step. In fact, a few early settlers in the western part of the States sent their children to Honolulu to be educated. Lahainaluna School, one of the oldest educational institutions in the United States, was established by the missionaries in 1831. The original schoolhouse was a grass hut.

The 117-year-old Kawaiahao Church in Honolulu is known as the "Westminster Abbey of Hawaii." It was here that state funerals for the Hawaiian kings and nobility were held and here the kings took their oaths of office. Since it was built, this church has been the ceremonial place for Hawaiian royalty. Today it is one of the few churches in which services are conducted in the Hawaiian language.

At first, discrimination did exist in the Hawaiian school system. Orientals and Polynesians were admitted only to certain schools, these always inferior to the schools attended by *haoles* in equipment, teaching staff and curriculum. Only after many years of disappointment and struggle have *all* the citizens of Hawaii achieved complete educational equality.

Today there are no "better" schools in Hawaii. Instead, there is a unified system which guarantees that a school in urban Honolulu and a school in a small rural village will provide equally good education. The Department of Public Instruction sets standards and provides teaching projects which apply to all. Teachers must have 5 years of training, and are paid uniform salaries regardless of the school at which they work. Proof that the early fight for equality has been truly won is the fact that in the 400 public and private schools in Hawaii, serving nearly 200,000 students, there is absolutely no racial segregation.

The worker shortage of a century ago also made its impression on Hawaii. The state maintains 4 public vocational schools, one on each of the four largest islands. These schools give students opportunities for on-the-job apprenticeships with local industries.

Staffing the elementary and high schools of the islands are 6,350 teachers. More than half of the high school graduates go on to colleges or universities, a substantial number to mainland

The first newspaper in the Pacific area, Kalama O Hawaii, was printed here in the 1830's. The house, called Hale Pa'i, was part of the Lahainaluna School on Maui, and is built out of slabs of coral rock. Today in Hawaii, there are 5 daily newspapers and 18 weekly or monthly publications.

institutions. They need not travel so far, however; right in Honolulu is an excellent university. Established by Act of Congress in 1907, the University of Hawaii has a campus of 710 acres. There is also a small branch in Hilo. It is a first-rate institution, accredited by the Western College Association. More than 7,000 students from all over the world come to study at the University of Hawaii. It is an important research base for marine biology, tropical agriculture, volcanology and sugar and pineapple technology. Quite appropriately, the University is also well known for its research and experimentation in the areas of race relations and international affairs.

WAY OF LIFE

Naturally, the Hawaiian way of life reflects the different cultures and nationalities of its people. Evidence of cultural diversity exists everywhere. Hawaiian houses combine Japanese simplicity of design, Polynesian love of relaxed, outdoor life, and the high living standards and modern conveniences that characterize the rest of the United States. Hawaiian food is similarly enriched in its variety by specialties from many countries. While American-style breakfasts and sandwich lunches are common, Japanese dishes like sukiyaki and shrimp tempura, and the rich range of Chinese cookery are very popular. Rice and fish remain the staple foods, but American influence has caused a sharp rise in the amount of meat consumed each year. Although *poi* is still widely eaten, the lavish Hawaiian *luau*, a feast featuring whole pig baked in an underground oven, steamed fish and at least a dozen more courses, is almost never prepared except for tourists.

The clothing worn in Hawaii is mainly American in design, but it also shows the influence of the various other peoples who live in the islands. Such accents as Chinese kimonos and Japanese sandals are very common. The *muumuu*, which is currently popular on the mainland, is actually a variation of the "Mother Hubbard," a loose, sack-like garment which the early missionaries imposed on the Polynesian women, who often wore nothing more than flowers in their hair.

Hawaiian music and dance also have their roots in many cultures. The hula, an ancient

The luau, *or feast, was far more common in Hawaii several centuries ago than it is today. Because they are so expensive to prepare,* luaus *are staged mostly for tourists. A typical menu of exotic foods includes roast pig cooked in an* imu *or underground oven, poi, which is eaten with the fingers, fish steamed and served in ti leaf parchment and coconut pudding.*

Luaus *can be small (above) or large (below).*

A hula dancer, dressed in a skirt made of tapa leaves and adorned with leis, keeps the rhythm supplied by a ukulele. Dancers like this one perform at the annual August Hula Festival, a gala dance competition.

Polynesian dance in which the hands tell a story while the hips and feet keep the rhythm, is perhaps the most popular dance. In August there is a special Hula Festival at which dancers of all ages display their skill. Almost every Hawaiian learns the hula in childhood; it is taught in some schools, and campaigning politicians find skill at the hula a real "must." However, the ukulele, which is often played to accompany this graceful dance, was brought to Hawaii by the Portuguese. Oddly, many of the ukuleles sold on the islands are actually manufactured in Pennsylvania. The word "ukulele" is Polynesian for "leaping fleas" and the instrument was so named because of the rapid movement of the fingers over its four strings. European influence extends to more serious music as well. Hawaii is proud of its 90-piece Honolulu Symphony Orchestra which offers year-round concerts, often featuring internationally known artists.

A vast complex of shops, a high-rise office building and numerous parking levels have been built year by year into the Ala Moana Shopping Center, said to be the largest in the world. A revolving restaurant atop the office building affords a spectacular panoramic view of all Honolulu.

Fishing by net is an ancient native skill. Here, a Hawaiian casts his net off the Kona coast on the south side of the island of Hawaii, where the fishing is the best in the state.

The geography of Hawaii, as well as its cultural makeup, is an important factor in shaping the Hawaiian way of life. Because of the mild climate, houses are built with large glass areas and open porches, or *lanais*. The exotic flowers and foliage growing almost wild in the islands provide lush gardens often extending right inside the houses. The warm weather is probably the main reason Hawaiians dress so casually. Sports clothes are worn everywhere, except in business offices and on very special occasions. Even in the cities, children rarely wear shoes.

Because the state is surrounded by water, fish is a staple food, and fishing a popular sport. The ancient Polynesians originated a community fishing party called a *hukilau*, and this net-fishing method is still in use today. Big game sportfishing is another well-loved pastime, especially off the Kona coast of the Big Island, where the waters abound in marlin and tuna of all varieties, as well as dolphins, wahoos, barracuda and bonito. Throughout the islands water sports of all kinds, swimming, surfriding, sailing and canoeing, are extremely popular. A look at Hawaii's beautiful beaches and warm clear waters tells why.

A third, and almost indefinable, aspect of the Hawaiian way of life is best summed up by the word *aloha*, which expresses the friendship, good fellowship and easy-going hospitality that characterize the islands. A week in October is set aside as Aloha Week, for special pageants, parades, canoe races, street dances and exhibits of ancient crafts. But the spirit of *aloha* can be felt in Hawaii on any day of the year. Closely entwined with island *aloha* is the lei. Again, although May 1 is designated as Lei Day, leis are used in abundance at greetings and fare-

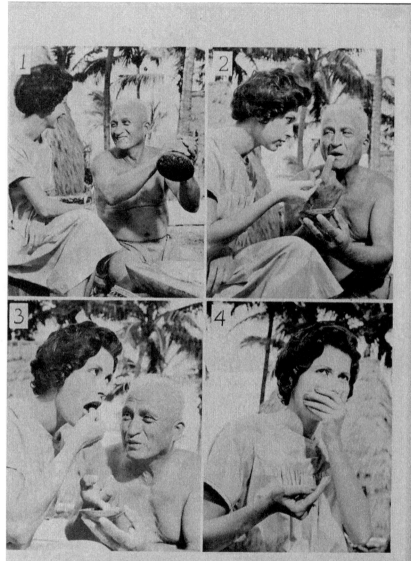

Step by step, a visitor to the islands samples poi, that staple Hawaiian food made from the taro root. Although she seems eager to taste poi, a rather pasty substance eaten with the fingers, this girl's final opinion seems negative. Although reactions vary, most inquisitive tasters don't take to poi immediately.

wells and on all other special occasions. Leis are even placed on graves, a custom which dates back to the ancient Polynesian nobility. Leis are presented in much the same way as mainlanders give corsages or bouquets. The only exception is that Hawaiian men, as well as women, wear leis.

One of the most striking uses to which leis are put occurs every June 11. This is Kamehameha Day, when Hawaiians recall the king who united the islands by draping his statue

Right: Dressed in a muumuu, *this Hawaiian girl makes the leis which she is selling. The two most popular kinds are the single vanda orchid lei, which is quite long-lasting, and the yellow plumeria, which has an especially wonderful fragrance.*

Below: Here is how poi, *the Hawaiian "staff of life," is made from the taro root. First it is steamed, then peeled and pounded. At the reconstructed village of Ulu Mau in Honolulu, a native demonstrates the way to prepare this starchy, pudding-like substance.*

45

with 40-foot leis, vivid floral wreaths reaching from his shoulders to the ground. On Kamehameha Day there is a parade as well, in which Hawaiians dress in the manner of the ancient Polynesian nobles, wearing feather capes and helmets. The making of these feather garments, a very intricate process, is actually a lost art today. There are some heirlooms of course, but the majority of capes worn in the annual parades are either made of flowers or paper. Most of the authentic feather garments are found only in museums such as the Bishop Museum in Honolulu, which is world famous for its Pacific collections and exhibits of Polynesian culture. A look into another museum, the Honolulu Academy of Arts with its fine collection of European, Oriental and Polynesian art, offers further proof of the contributions to Hawaiian culture by the many different peoples who have made the Hawaiian way of life their own.

The Honolulu Academy of Arts is a treasure house of Pacificana. In its galleries and landscaped patios, modern Polynesian paintings, sculptures and ancient wood carvings, as well as European and Oriental art, are displayed. The portal of the Academy is guarded by a pair of Hawaiian gods carved out of giant fern trees.

The catamaran, a modern version of the ancient Polynesian outrigger canoe, is a familiar sight at Waikiki. Billed as the fastest craft in Hawaiian waters, the catamaran comes right to Waikiki Beach to pick up vacationers for a ride under sail to Diamond Head, and back with the waves to the Beach.

Below: Surfriding is extremely popular with natives and tourists alike. Standing on surfboards, riders skilfully skim the waves.

These Hawaiians are preparing to do some underwater swimming with masks and flippers to see what lies under the waters off Hanalei Beach, on Kauai. It was at this beach that much of the filming of the motion picture "South Pacific" was done.

Waikiki's Kuhio Beach, named after one of Hawaii's most beloved members of royalty, is bounded on one side by resort hotels which have been built since the end of World War II.

Both visitors and native Hawaiians participate in a net fishing party by torch light. While these men examine the catch, onlookers stand by in gaily printed muumuus and sport shirts.

An unusual sport is horseback riding along the surf at Hamoa Beach, Hana.

49

A variety of hats awaits the lady at the Waikiki shopping area.

A hula dancer, a palm tree, a grassy beach, and, beyond, the sea—a scene which is typical of Hawaii. The graceful, expressive hula is a difficult dance to master. Its movements tell a story in which the position of the arms and hands is especially important.

PROPERTY OF
DELPHOS ATTENDANCE CENTER

Hawaiian sugar cane is allowed to mature for 22 to 24 months, during which time it grows to a height of 15 to 20 feet. These men are taking samples in order to test a new variety of cane.

4. THE ECONOMY

Sugar, tourists, pineapple and national defence activity are what keep the islands of Hawaii in thriving economic condition. For nearly a century sugar has held first place as the major product of Hawaii, and for many years accounted for half the total income earned by all Hawaiian exports.

No one knows for sure just how sugar cane first got to the islands. Legends tell of a Chinese junk, blown off its course and shipwrecked near Hawaii. The sugar industry, however, got its start in 1835 at Koloa on the island of Kauai, when three New Englanders operating as Ladd & Company signed a lease with King Kamehameha III for 980 acres of land. Twelve of these acres they planted with sugar cane, and two years later exported their first crop, 2.1 tons of raw sugar and 2,700

51

MINNEAPOLIS JUNIOR HIGH

Above: Irrigation is very important to the growing of sugar. Nearly one-fourth of all the money invested in the industry is used for this purpose. A single plantation uses 145 million gallons of water a day, three times the amount used by the city of Honolulu. Shown here, is an irrigation ditch running through a field of cane.

Below: Modern scientific techniques have helped make the sugar industry a year-round operation. Here, large tractors pull harrows which break up the soil and prepare it for planting. The "seeds" used to plant sugar cane are lengths of stalk, from 1 to 3 feet long.

gallons of molasses. Today at Koloa more than 8,000 acres are used to grow sugar cane, and 35,000 tons of raw sugar are exported each year. From the total of 27 sugar plantations throughout the state (located on the islands of Kauai, Oahu, Maui and Hawaii), more than one million tons of raw sugar are produced yearly. Sugar grown in Hawaii represents one-fourth of the sugar produced in the United States, one-ninth of the total American consumption, and about 3 per cent of the entire world production. The raw sugar produced in Hawaii is exported in bulk form on specially designed ships which transport it to the mainland for refining. About 5 per cent of the sugar is refined in Hawaii itself for local use.

The Chinese and Japanese sugar workers of a century ago would hardly recognize today's plantations, for they are highly mechanized. The preparation of soil, fertilizing, planting and harvesting are all done by machines as is a large part of the irrigation process. Irrigation, by the way, is vital to the sugar industry. Even though soil and climate conditions in Hawaii are so good that the yield of cane per acre is larger than anywhere else in the world, 2,000 tons of water are still required to produce one ton of sugar. Despite mechanization, the sugar industry today continues to be a major source of employment, providing work for some 16,000 persons.

Sugar cane in Hawaii is burned before it is harvested. Years ago a fire swept the cane fields and, to the amazement of all, only the leaves and undergrowth were destroyed, while stalks were left clean and standing. Tests showed no appreciable loss in sugar content, and since it is far easier to harvest the cane, which is almost junglelike in growth, without its leaves, burning the cane just prior to cutting it is now a standard practice.

The cane grab is the machine used to harvest the major portion of the Hawaiian sugar crop. After the cane is cut, it grows again from the old root system without a new planting of seed. This growth is called a "ratoon" crop. From 2 to 4 ratoon crops are obtained from each original planting.

One of Hawaii's 27 sugar mills stands in a field of sugar cane. Sugar companies like this one are owned by more than 14,000 stockholders.

Below: Plantation workers are generally furnished with free homes, as well as land for vegetable and flower gardens like these at the Oahu plantation overlooking Pearl Harbor. In the foreground is a small avocado tree.

New types of cane are bred by plant geneticists at this research institution. They are trying to develop strains which will yield the highest possible percentage of sugar.

The Hawaiian Sugar Planter's Association, a nonprofit organization jointly financed by the sugar plantations, has established an outstanding agricultural experiment station. The scientists at work here are engaged in their constant search for new varieties of cane that will better resist drought and insects.

A passenger ship steams past Diamond Head out of Honolulu Harbor. Each year major steamship lines and airlines bring about 1,500,000 visitors to Hawaii from all over the world.

The modern Princess Kaiulani Hotel in Honolulu is built on the grounds where its namesake grew up, paraded her pet peacocks and became a friend of the Scottish writer Robert Louis Stevenson. He called her "my little princess." Like many Hawaiian hotels, the Princess Kaiulani has a private beach as well as its own swimming pool, set in a lush private garden.

56

Long rivalling sugar as the number one industry of the islands, the tourist business has, as many economists predicted, finally taken over the lead. About 3,000,000 visitors from all over the world came to Hawaii in 1974. At least 18,000 employees and 10,000 rooms in modern hotels are dedicated to their comfort. With steamships docking almost daily, and an average of 10 passenger planes a day landing at Honolulu International Airport, getting to Hawaii from almost anywhere in the world presents no problem. And although the islands do not offer bargain holidays, the era when only millionaires could vacation there is well over. The great majority of tourists in Hawaii today are middle-income Americans.

The great tourist attraction of Hawaii, of course, is the promise of a true tropical atmosphere without language problems or currency difficulties. The sparkling beaches, awesome volcanoes, gentle climate and exotic flowers all lure visitors to the Islands. So, too, does Hawaii's reputation for friendliness and hospitality. Mainlanders particularly, perhaps with some envy, enjoy the Hawaiian *hoomanawanui*, its easy way of life. Whatever their reasons for coming, Hawaii welcomes them, for vacationers on the Islands spend huge sums every year in addition to their transport costs.

The pineapple industry, last of Hawaii's "big three," is found on five islands: Oahu, Maui, Molokai, Lanai and Kauai. Nine pineapple companies operate 13 plantations, with a total acreage of 76,700, or about one-third as much land as is used by the sugar industry.

The first written mention of the pineapple in Hawaii was in 1813, though as with sugar cane, we do not know exactly when the fruit was first introduced to the islands. The foundations for the present pineapple industry were laid by Captain John Kidwell, an English horticulturist who was trying to find a better-tasting fruit than the pineapple native to Hawaii. In 1886 he imported from Jamaica 1,000 plants of the smooth cayenne variety, the kind of pineapple principally grown in Hawaii today. Because this superior-tasting fruit did not keep well on the long voyage from Honolulu to San Francisco, Kidwell made the all-important decision that if pineapple were to become significant in Hawaii's economy, it would have to be preserved in cans. Although his attempt at canning, begun in 1892, was not commercially successful, he was, of course, correct. It remained for a young Harvard graduate, who came to Hawaii from Boston in 1899, to perfect the canning process. This young man was James D. Dole, a cousin of Sanford Dole. He became the real pioneer of the industry with his organization of the Hawaiian Pineapple Company. In 1901, his first year of business, Dole packaged about 1,800 cases of canned pineapple.

Today, production from Hawaii's nine canneries averages 29 million cases of fruit and juice per year, which represents 80 per cent of all the pineapple sold in the United States. The industry employs 10,000 persons on a year-round basis, and another 12,000 temporary workers.

Pineapple is planted with cuttings from another pineapple. These can be slips taken from the base of the fruit, "suckers" cut from lower down on the stem, or crowns from the top of the fruit, as illustrated here. The roots are covered with black mulch paper which not only holds in heat and moisture, but also keeps down the growth of weeds.

Pineapples need nearly two years to mature fully, at which time they are about the size of a football. Fifteen months after the planting, buds 2 to 3 inches long sprout in the middle of the plant. Then, dozens of little pink and blue flowers, each lasting only a day, blossom around the outside of this tiny pineapple. The plants here, growing on Kauai, still have several months to go before they will be ripe.

This unusual machine is a pineapple harvester. The long arm is a conveyor belt which carries the fruit to a bin or truck specially designed to handle it without bruising. The fruit is then rushed to the cannery. Shortly after harvesting, planting material is collected, and a small number of "suckers" are left to bear fruit a second year. But after the second crop has been harvested, the plants are ploughed under and the field is prepared for a new planting.

Paniolas, *or Hawaiian cowboys, tend cattle on the huge Parker Ranch, located near Mauna Loa on the island of Hawaii.*

Although not in the same rank with sugar, tourists and pineapple, cattle ranching makes its own healthy bid as a major industry of Hawaii, and is growing more and more important every year. In 1793, Captain George Vancouver first introduced cattle and sheep from California, and now there are 80 ranches and 100,000 head of livestock on the islands. The largest ranch, which is in fact the second largest in the world, is the Parker Ranch on the island of Hawaii. John Palmer Parker was an American sailor who jumped ship in 1815 and stayed on the islands to hunt wild cattle for King Kamehameha I. Parker married a Polynesian woman, acquired title to land in the Waimea Plateau on Hawaii island and founded a family which for over a century has built up herds of beef cattle from the original wild stock. The Parker Ranch totals 300,000 acres and boasts the largest herd of registered Hereford cattle in the world.

Apart from these ranches and the sugar and pineapple plantations, large farms are very rare in Hawaii. Most of the 5,000 Hawaiian farms are small, family-operated homesteads of only 1 to 5 acres. On these are raised poultry, eggs, vegetables, melons, alfalfa and other cattle feeds, fruit, flowers, foliage and macadamia nuts, which have lately become very popular on the United States mainland.

Somewhat larger, although still seldom over 100 acres, are the farms devoted to coffee-growing. The main coffee-growing region is the Kona district of the island of Hawaii, where some 7,000 acres are divided into 800 or 900 farms for the cultivation of this crop. Coffee was first grown on Hawaii in 1817, and now an appreciable quantity of milled coffee is produced yearly.

Until now we have been primarily concerned with the agricultural industries of Hawaii, and indeed, prior to World War II the islands had maintained a largely agricultural society. With the advent of the war, however, a major change took place in the economic life of Hawaii. After the bombing of Pearl Harbor in 1941, Honolulu was turned into a military camp. Defence work engaged 75,000 people, and half a million military troops were stationed on the islands. Honolulu is still the focus of American defence in the Pacific, but many of the factories

59

Rice and taro, two of the most important foods in the Hawaiian menu, are grown on small farms like these in the Hanalei valley on the island of Kauai.

A true picture of the Hawaiian economy must, of course, include occupations carried on outside the cities. One of the most important of these is fishing. Here, an elderly Japanese repairs his fish nets.

The heart of industry and commerce is the capital city of Honolulu, on the island of Oahu. Palm trees which line these avenues lend an exotic air even to the bustling business section.

which were built for wartime uses are now utilized for the manufacture of a variety of peacetime products.

This variety, in fact, is somewhat surprising. Over 142 different products are manufactured in Hawaii, ranging from awnings, baskets and chemicals, through machinery and metals, right down the alphabet to Venetian blinds. With nearly 550 manufacturing companies in operation (240 in food processing and related activities, and 125 others in printing, publishing and clothing manufacture), the rate of employment in Hawaii is generally very high. Along with the factories, banking and insurance

The building boom on Oahu is well illustrated by the dozens of high-rise structures erected back of Waikiki Beach in recent years.

companies and a major construction trade help keep the islands prosperous.

Small crafts, although less vital to the state's economy, are of interest mainly for their ancient origin. Notable among them are glass etching, textile decorating, furniture making, jewelry, weaving and woodworking.

The production of all these Hawaiian goods would hardly be meaningful if there were not a wide market for them. The United States mainland is of course the major trading place, as it has been since 1875 when the Reciprocity Treaty established practically free trade between the islands and the United States. Other countries pick up their share of Hawaiian trade

as well, for Honolulu is located midway between San Francisco and Tokyo, Sydney, Australia and Fairbanks, Alaska. Even 100 years ago this excellent port was the most important base of the whaling trade. Today more than ever, Honolulu, and thus the state of Hawaii, maintains its position as the commercial crossroads of the Pacific Ocean.

The increase in population on Oahu and the flourishing tourist industry have brought about a building boom there. Conservationists are afraid that Oahu's leisurely life may soon be affected by the same urban problems that plague the mainland states.

Visitors and Islanders alike enjoy paddling outrigger canoes and riding surfboards at Waikiki. Surf-boards rent at nominal rates and canoe rides are available hourly, with native steersmen in charge.

Kalakaua Avenue in Waikiki beckons the stroller to window-shop or sample foods from many lands at the International Market Place. The modern Waikiki Business Plaza, topped with a revolving restaurant, is in the background.

INDEX

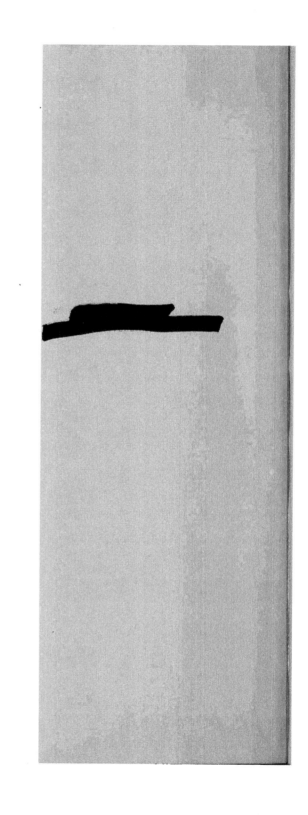

DELPHOS
LIBRARY

Printed in the USA
CPSIA information can be obtained
at www.ICGtesting.com
LVHW020552051023
759046LV00004B/14

9 781014 110510